Dear Parent:
Your child's love of reading starts here!

Every child learns to read in a different way and at his or her own speed. Some go back and forth between reading levels and read favorite books again and again. Others read through each level in order. You can help your young reader improve and become more confident by encouraging his or her own interests and abilities. From books your child reads with you to the first books he or she reads alone, there are I Can Read Books for every stage of reading:

SHARED READING
Basic language, word repetition, and whimsical illustrations, ideal for sharing with your emergent reader

BEGINNING READING
Short sentences, familiar words, and simple concepts for children eager to read on their own

READING WITH HELP
Engaging stories, longer sentences, and language play for developing readers

READING ALONE
Complex plots, challenging vocabulary, and high-interest topics for the independent reader

ADVANCED READING
Short paragraphs, chapters, and exciting themes for the perfect bridge to chapter books

I Can Read Books have introduced children to the joy of reading since 1957. Featuring award-winning authors and illustrators and a fabulous cast of beloved characters, I Can Read Books set the standard for beginning readers.

A lifetime of discovery begins with the magical words "I Can Read!"

Visit www.icanread.com for information
on enriching your child's reading experience.

I Can Read Book® is a trademark of HarperCollins Publishers.

Digger the Dinosaur and the Cake Mistake Copyright © 2011 by HarperCollins Publishers All rights reserved. Manufactured in the U.S.A. No part of this book may be used or reproduced in any manner whatsoever without written permission except in the case of brief quotations embodied in critical articles and reviews. For information address HarperCollins Children's Books, a division of HarperCollins Publishers, 195 Broadway, New York, NY 10007. www.icanread.com

Library of Congress catalog card number: 2013935040
ISBN 978-0-06-222224-4 (trade bdg.) — ISBN 978-0-06-222223-7 (pbk.)

18 19 20   LSCC   15 14 13   ❖   First Edition

Digger the Dinosaur

and the Cake Mistake

By Rebecca Kai Dotlich
Pictures by Gynux

HARPER
An Imprint of HarperCollinsPublishers

Digger hopped off his bike.

Today was a great day.

It was the big dino party!

Digger raced to the door.
Momasaur and Dadasaur
were waiting.

DINO PARTY HERE

"Digger!" said Momasaur.
"I'm glad you're home.
It's time to get the cake."

"Got it!" Digger said.

He hopped into the car.

Dadasaur drove into town.

He turned left.

Then he turned right.

"I don't see a cake shop,"
said Dadasaur.
"Can you call Mom?"

Digger dialed Momasaur's number.

"Hello? Hello?" Digger asked.

"Did we pass what?"

"Did you pass a park?"
Momasaur asked.

"A shark!?" yelled Digger.

"PARK," said Momasaur.

"Oh!" said Digger.

"Park! Yes we did."

"Do you see the blue house?"
Momasaur asked.

"STOP!" said Digger.

Dadasaur stopped the car.

Digger and Dad got out.

"The new house!"

said Digger.

"No, Digger,"
said Momasaur.
"BLUE, not new."
"Got it," said Digger.

"I still don't see
a cake shop,"
said Dadasaur.

"I know!" said Digger.
"I ride bikes here with Stego.
We saw a cake shop."

Digger pointed to the right.
"Then we need to brake,"
said Dadasaur.

"We need a CAKE,"
said Digger.
Dadasaur roared.

"Good thing you came
with me," said Dadasaur.
"Very good thing,"
said Digger.

Digger went into the shop.

He came back with a big cake.

"Next stop, home!" he said.

"We take a right here,"
said Dadasaur.
"A BITE here?!"
asked Digger.

"Don't you dare,"
said Dadasaur.
"Got it," said Digger.

Dadasaur and Digger roared.